ARIZONA CARDINALS

BY JOSH ANDERSON

Stride
An Imprint of The Child's World®
childsworld.com

The Child's World
childsworld.com

Published by The Child's World®
800-599-READ • www.childsworld.com

Photography Credits
Cover: © Wesley Hitt / Stringer / Getty Images; page 1: © Africa Studio / Shutterstock; page 3: © Ezra Shaw / Staff / Getty Images; page 5: © Will Vragovic / Stringer / Getty Images; page 6: © George Rose / Stringer / Getty Images; page 9: © Ralph Freso / Stringer / Getty Images; page 10: © Robert Laberge / Staff / Getty Images; page 11: © stevezmina1 / Getty Images; page 12: © Christian Petersen / Staff / Getty Images; page 12: © Sean M. Haffey / Staff / Getty Images; page 13: © Jamie Squire / Staff / Getty Images; page 13: © Abbie Parr / Stringer / Getty Images; page 14: © Norm Hall / Stringer / Getty Images; page 15: © Christian Petersen / Staff / Getty Images; page 16: © Streeter Lecka / Staff / Getty Images; page 16: © Dman41689 / Wikimedia; page 17: © Otto Greule Jr / Stringer / Getty Images; page 17: © NFHOF / Associated Press; page 18: © Mike Powell / Staff / Getty Images; page 18: © Irwin Dougherty / UPI Photo Service / Newscom; page 19: © Christian Petersen / Staff / Getty Images; page 19: © Andy Lyons / Staff / Getty Images; page 20: © Christian Petersen / Staff / Getty Images; page 20: © Christian Petersen / Staff / Getty Images; page 21: © Christian Petersen / Staff / Getty Images; page 21: © Steph Chambers / Staff / Getty Images; page 22: © Gregory Shamus / Staff / Getty Images; page 23: © Tom Hauck / Staff / Getty Images; page 23: © stevezmina1 / Getty Images; page 25: © Jamie Squire / Staff / Getty Images; page 26: © Norm Hall / Stringer / Getty Images; page 29: © Arnie Sachs/ZUMA Press / Newscom

ISBN Information
9781503857711 (Reinforced Library Binding)
9781503860384 (Portable Document Format)
9781503861749 (Online Multi-user eBook)
9781503863101 (Electronic Publication)

LCCN 2021952618

Printed in the United States of America

BRINGING THE WORLD TO YOUNG READERS 1968

TABLE OF CONTENTS

GO CARDINALS!

The Arizona Cardinals compete in the National Football **League's** (NFL's) National Football Conference (NFC). They play in the NFC West **division**, along with the Los Angeles Rams, San Francisco 49ers, and Seattle Seahawks. The Cardinals are one of the oldest **franchises** in sports. They've been a part of professional football for more than 100 years. The team played in several cities before finding a permanent home in Phoenix. Let's learn more about the Cardinals!

NFC WEST DIVISION

Arizona Cardinals

Los Angeles Rams

San Francisco 49ers

Seattle Seahawks

THE ARIZONA CARDINALS WERE THE ONLY TEAM TO WIN THEIR FIRST SEVEN GAMES DURING THE 2021 SEASON.

BECOMING THE CARDINALS

The NFL began play in 1920, but it was called the American Professional Football Association (APFA) until 1922. Of the 14 original teams in the league, only the Bears and Cardinals still exist. At that time, though, the Cardinals played in Chicago, Illinois. The team moved to St. Louis, Missouri, in 1960. They moved again in 1988 to Arizona, where they've been ever since. In 1994, the team changed its name from the Phoenix Cardinals to the Arizona Cardinals.

QUARTERBACK NEIL LOMAX LED THE TEAM TO 47 VICTORIES BETWEEN 1981 AND 1988.

BY THE NUMBERS

The Cardinals have played in **ONE** Super Bowl.

14
players in the Pro Football **Hall of Fame**

489
points scored by the team in 2015—a Cardinals record!

13
wins in 2015—most in team history!

TIGHT END DAN ARNOLD SCORED A TOUCHDOWN IN A 2019 GAME AGAINST THE CLEVELAND BROWNS, HELPING THE CARDINALS TO A VICTORY.

CARDINALS PLAYERS ENTER THE FIELD ON GAME DAYS THROUGH A GIANT INFLATABLE CARDINAL TUNNEL.

GAME DAY

The Cardinals play their home games at State Farm **Stadium** in Glendale, Arizona. They've played there since 2006. On game days, State Farm Stadium holds 63,400 fans. It is the only stadium in the league with a retractable grass field that can be removed and kept outside of the building when not in use. This allows the stadium to be used for other events. And it allows the field to get the proper amount of sunlight in Arizona's desert climate.

We're Famous!

The Cardinals achieved fame on the big screen in the 1996 movie *Jerry Maguire*. Actor Cuba Gooding Jr. won an Academy Award for playing Rod Tidwell, a Cardinals wide receiver. Hoping for a new contract, Tidwell says one of the most famous lines in movie history: "Show me the money!"

UNIFORM

RED

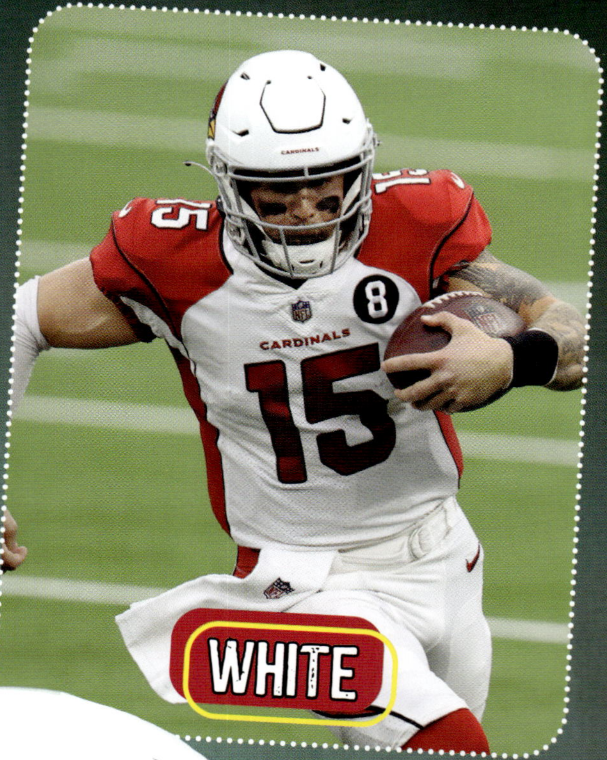

WHITE

Truly Weird

Running back Thomas Jones was having his best season in 2002 when he received an unfortunate phone call. Jones reached for the phone but accidentally hit a countertop so hard that it broke his hand. The crazy injury resulted in Jones missing the final seven games of the season.

Alternate Jersey

Sometimes teams wear an alternate jersey that is different from their home and away jerseys. It might be a bright color or have a unique theme. The Cardinals wore all black twice in 2020. The new look proved unlucky, though. The Cardinals lost both games.

CARDINALS PLAYERS SOMETIMES JUMP INTO THE STANDS TO CELEBRATE A TOUCHDOWN WITH CHEERING FANS.

TEAM SPIRIT

Going to a game at State Farm Stadium can be loads of fun. The game starts out with a blast from the Big Red Siren. The siren makes a wailing noise as the Cardinals run out from the locker room. Sometimes celebrity guests are invited to State Farm Stadium to sound the siren. No game in Arizona would be complete without the Cardinals cheerleaders or Big Red, the team's mascot. Big Red is a giant cardinal who's been entertaining the crowd at Cardinals games since 1998!

BIG RED

HEROES OF HISTORY

Anquan Boldin

Wide Receiver | 2003–2009

Boldin ranks ninth in NFL history with 1,076 catches in his career. He's fourth in Cardinals history with 7,520 yards receiving. The three-time **Pro Bowler** was a key part of the Cardinals' run to the Super Bowl during the 2008 season.

Richard "Night Train" Lane

Cornerback | 1954–1959

Night Train Lane ranks fourth all-time in interceptions. The fierce tackler holds the single-season interception record with 14. Lane is a member of the Pro Football Hall of Fame, and he was selected as one of the NFL's 100 greatest players of all time.

Aeneas Williams

Cornerback | 1991–2000

An eight-time Pro Bowler, Williams led the Cardinals in interceptions seven times. He ranks fifth all-time with nine interceptions returned for a **touchdown**. Williams was known for his incredible hustle on the field. He was inducted into the Pro Football Hall of Fame in 2014.

Larry Wilson

Safety | 1960–1972

Wilson is known as the player who made the "safety blitz" popular. When he wasn't attacking the quarterback, he intercepted 52 passes in his career. Wilson led the league in interceptions with 10 in 1966. The eight-time Pro Bowler is a member of the Pro Football Hall of Fame.

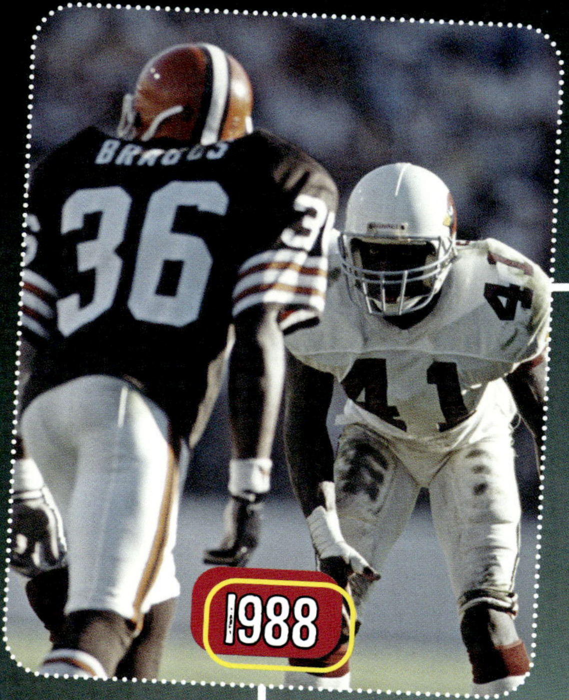

A new era of Cardinals football begins. The team moves from St. Louis, Missouri, and plays its first season in Arizona.

The Cardinals defeat the San Diego Chargers 16–13 and earn a trip to the **playoffs**. It's their first winning season since 1984.

BIG DAYS

JANUARY 16, 2016

The Cardinals defeat the Green Bay Packers 26–20 in a playoff game. The win sends Arizona to the NFC Conference Championship Game.

APRIL 25, 2019

With the first overall selection in the 2019 NFL Draft, the Cardinals select quarterback Kyler Murray.

MODERN-DAY MARVELS

Budda Baker

Safety | Debut: 2017

Baker is one of only two Cardinals ever to earn three trips to the Pro Bowl before his 25th birthday. His 104 solo tackles led the NFL in 2019. Considered one of the best safeties in the league, Baker was chosen as a team captain in 2020.

Zach Ertz

Tight End | Debut: 2021

Ertz played more than eight seasons with the Philadelphia Eagles. He joined the Cardinals in the middle of the 2021 season. In 11 games with the team in 2021, he gained 574 receiving yards. He also scored three touchdowns. Ertz has been chosen for the Pro Bowl three times.

DeAndre Hopkins

Wide Receiver | Debut: 2020

Fans were thrilled to welcome five-time Pro Bowler Hopkins ahead of the 2020 season. In his first season with the Cardinals, Hopkins set a franchise record with 115 catches. He also finished third in the NFL with 1,407 receiving yards.

Kyler Murray

Quarterback | Debut: 2019

Chosen by the Cardinals with the first pick in the NFL Draft in 2019, Murray won the NFL's Offensive **Rookie** of the Year award. His 61 combined touchdowns (passing and rushing) were the third-most ever in a player's first two seasons.

LARRY FITZGERALD WAS A MEMBER OF THE CARDINALS FOR 17 YEARS.

THE GOAT

GREATEST OF ALL TIME

LARRY FITZGERALD

Fitzgerald is widely considered one of the greatest receivers in football history. He ranks second all-time with 1,432 catches and 17,492 receiving yards. In 2019, Fitzgerald was one of only four active players named to the NFL's list of the 100 greatest players of all time. He was elected to the Pro Bowl 11 times and helped lead the Cardinals to the playoffs four times. His 30 catches and seven touchdowns in the 2008 postseason are both NFL records.

FAN FAVORITE

Pat Tillman–Safety

1998–2001

Tillman became a beloved figure to fans across the NFL for what he did off the field. In 2002, he turned down a contract offer from the Cardinals and enlisted in the US Army. He wanted to serve his country during Operation Enduring Freedom in Afghanistan. Sadly, Tillman lost his life during his time in the army.

THE BIG GAME

JANUARY 18, 2009 – NFC CHAMPIONSHIP GAME

The Cardinals came into their NFC Championship Game matchup with the Philadelphia Eagles hoping to earn their first trip to the Super Bowl. In 2008, the Cardinals had a great offense. But the Eagles had one of the league's top defenses. The Cardinals took an early 24–6 lead when quarterback Kurt Warner threw three touchdown passes to wide receiver Larry Fitzgerald. But the Eagles came back and took a 25–24 lead in the fourth quarter. With less than three minutes to go, Kurt Warner found running back Tim Hightower in the end zone. The Cardinals won 32–25 and went on to play in Super Bowl 42.

RUNNING BACK EDGERRIN JAMES HELPED THE CARDINALS EARN A TRIP TO SUPER BOWL 42.

BRUCE ARIANS COACHED THE CARDINALS TO 49 VICTORIES. HE LED THE TEAM TO THE PLAYOFFS TWICE.

AMAZING FEATS

4,671 Passing Yards

In 2015 by
QUARTERBACK
Carson Palmer

16 Rushing Touchdowns

In 2016 by
RUNNING BACK
David Johnson

19 Sacks

In 2019 by
LINEBACKER
Chandler Jones

1,605 Rushing Yards

In 1979 by
RUNNING BACK
Ottis Anderson

ALL-TIME BEST

PASSING YARDS

Jim Hart
34,639

Neil Lomax
22,771

Jake Plummer
17,622

RUSHING YARDS

Ottis Anderson
7,999

Stump Mitchell
4,649

Jim Otis
3,863

RECEIVING YARDS

Larry Fitzgerald
17,492

Roy Green
8,496

Jackie Smith
7,918

SACKS*

Chandler Jones
71.5

Curtis Greer
69.5

Freddie Joe Nunn
66.5

SCORING

Jim Bakken
1,380

Larry Fitzgerald
732

Neil Rackers
699

INTERCEPTIONS

Larry Wilson
52

Aeneas Williams
46

Roger Wehrli
40

*unofficial before 1982

OTTIS ANDERSON SCORED 51 TOUCHDOWNS DURING HIS EIGHT SEASONS WITH THE CARDINALS.

GLOSSARY

division (dih-VIZSH-un): a group of teams within the NFL who play each other more frequently and compete for the best record

Hall of Fame (HAHL of FAYM): a museum in Canton, Ohio, that honors the best players in NFL history.

league (LEEG): an organization of sports teams that compete against each other

playoffs (PLAY-ahfs): a series of games after the regular season that decides which two teams play in the Super Bowl

Pro Bowl (PRO BOWL): the NFL's All-Star Game where the best players in the league compete

rookie (RUH-kee): a player playing in his first season

sack (SAK): when a quarterback is tackled behind the line of scrimmage before he can throw the ball

stadium (STAY-dee-uhm): a building with a field and seats for fans where teams play

Super Bowl (SOO-puhr BOWL): the championship game of the NFL, played between the winners of the AFC and the NFC

touchdown (TUTCH-down): a play in which the ball is brought into the other team's end zone, resulting in six points

FIND OUT MORE

IN THE LIBRARY

Bulgar, Beth and Mark Bechtel. *My First Book of Football.* New York, NY: Time Inc. Books, 2015.

Jacobs, Greg. *The Everything Kids' Football Book, 7th Edition*. Avon, MA: Adams Media, 2021.

Sports Illustrated Kids. *The Greatest Football Teams of All Time*. New York, NY: Time Inc. Books, 2018.

Wyner, Zach. *Arizona Cardinals*. New York, NY: AV2, 2020.

ON THE WEB

Visit our website for links about the Arizona Cardinals:
childsworld.com/links

Note to parents, teachers, and librarians: We routinely verify our web links to make sure they are safe and active sites. Encourage your readers to check them out!

INDEX

ABOUT THE AUTHOR

Josh Anderson has published over 50 books for children and young adults. His two boys are the greatest joys in his life. Hobbies include coaching his sons in youth basketball, no-holds-barred games of Apples to Apples, and taking long family walks. His favorite NFL team is a secret he'll never share!